Basic Skills

Story Elements

Learning About the Components of Stories to Deepen Comprehension

Grades 1-2

**By
Karen Clemens Warrick**

Cover Artist
Laura Zarrin

**Inside Illustrations by
Becky Radtke**

Published by Instructional Fair • TS Denison
an imprint of

About the Author

Karen Clemens Warrick holds a bachelor of science degree from Ball State University as well as a master's degree in elementary education from Arizona State University. After fifteen years of teaching, Karen became an author of both educational materials and biographies for children. She is a member of the Society of Children's Book Writers and Illustrators, and has conducted writing workshops for teachers. Karen lives with her husband, Jim, in Prescott, Arizona.

Credits

Author: Karen Clemens Warrick
Cover Artist: Laura Zarrin
Cover Design: Matthew Van Zomeren
Inside Illustrations: Becky Radtke
Project Director/Editor: Kathryn Wheeler
Editors: Linda Triemstra, Sara Bierling
Graphic Layout: Tracy L. Wesorick

McGraw-Hill Children's Publishing
A Division of The McGraw·Hill Companies

Published by Instructional Fair • TS Denison
An imprint of McGraw-Hill Children's Publishing
Copyright © 2001 McGraw-Hill Children's Publishing

Limited Reproduction Permission: Permission to duplicate these materials is limited to the person for whom they are purchased. Reproduction for an entire school or school district is unlawful and strictly prohibited.

Send all inquiries to:
McGraw-Hill Children's Publishing
3195 Wilson Drive NW
Grand Rapids, Michigan 49544

All Rights Reserved • Printed in the United States of America

Story Elements—grades 1-2
ISBN: 0-7424-0102-2

About the Book

Story Elements is designed to introduce young readers and writers to tools that authors use as they create stories. The activities explore the concepts of character, setting, problem (conflict), and plot. The book is divided into sections for each concept. Within each section, the activities progress from easiest to more challenging. In addition, some exercises incorporate a cross-curricular element to help reinforce reading skills for other subject areas.

Once students have been introduced to these basic concepts, reinforce their understanding by identifying characters, settings, problems, and plot in stories shared during storytime and in reading groups.

Table of Contents

Characters Tell the Story (character)......4	Where Are You? (setting) 24
Happy or Sad? (character) 5	Birthday Money (setting) 25–26
It's My Story (character) 6	Friends on the Map (setting) 27–28
The Hunters (character).....................7	Science Poster (setting) 29
Name That Character! (character) 8	What's the Problem? (problem) 30
Go, Characters, Go! (character) 9	The Dog and the Bone (problem)........31
Picture This (character) 10	Beach Trouble (problem) 32
Trading Toys (character) 11–12	Lots of Problems (problem) 33
Who Said That? (character) 13	I Know an Old Lady (problem) 34–35
Time for Dusty (character) 14	Oh, No! (problem) 36
The Lion and the Mouse (character) 15–16	A Gift for Mama (problem)................37
The Setting (setting) 17	Who's Lost? (problem) 38
In the Picture (setting) 18	The Big Problem (problem) 39–40
Setting the Mood (setting) 19	The Snowman (mixed elements)..........41
Out of Place (setting) 20	Putting It All Together (plot)..........42–43
Get the Picture (setting).....................21	Casey the Cowgirl (plot) 44–45
It's About Time (setting) 22	It's the End (mixed elements) 46
Time Travel (setting) 23	Answer Key 47–48

Name _____

Characters Tell the Story

character

> Read about **characters**. Then answer the questions.

Every story has characters.

A character can be a  or  who runs and plays and goes to school.

Or a story character can be a  or a  .

Maybe the character is a  or a ___ .

Sometimes characters feel happy. Sometimes they feel sad.

Reading about characters we like can be fun.

Look at the books. Draw a line to the characters from each book.

1. Little Red Riding Hood

2. Goldilocks and the Three Bears

3. Cinderella

> **Try this:** Draw your favorite character.

Name _____

Happy or Sad?

How does the character feel? Draw a or a .

character

1.

2.

3.

4.

5.

6.

5

© Instructional Fair • TS Denison   IF5635 Story Elements

Name _____

character

It's My Story

Circle the character's name. Then choose the best title for each story.

1. Ramon

   Lisa

   Ruff

Lisa Draws   Lisa Makes a Mask

2. Ramon

   Lisa

   Ruff

Ramon Flies a Kite   Ramon Plays

3. Ramon

   Lisa

   Ruff

Ruff Digs   Ruff Finds a Bone

Try this: Write a story about one of these characters.

Name _____

character

The Hunters

Read the story. Then answer the questions.

 asked her  for a . They poked holes in the lid. Then  walked to the .  was in the , too. He had a  and a little . and wanted to find something to show at .

They both found something. They both had fun on their hunt.

Circle a picture to answer each question.

1. Who took the  to the ?

2. Who had a ?

3. Who took a to the ?

4. Who caught a  in the ?

5. Who caught a  in the 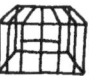?

6. Who had something to show at ?

© Instructional Fair • TS Denison   IF5635 *Story Elements*

Name _____

character

Name That Character!

Read the story. Ask your teacher if you need help.

1. He hopped out of the oven.
   He ran and ran as fast as he could.
   No one could catch him.

2. He climbed up and up the water spout.
   The rain fell and washed him out.
   Later, he climbed again.

3. She wanted to bake bread.
   She asked the other animals to help.
   No one would help,
   but they wanted to eat!

4. He was very hungry and very big.
   He wanted to eat three little pigs.
   He tried to blow their house down.

these pictures out.  each character next to the right story.

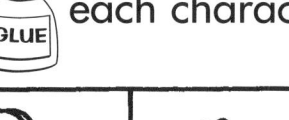

© Instructional Fair • TS Denison   IF5635 Story Elements

Name _____

character

Go, Characters, Go!

Draw a line from each sentence to its picture. Write the action word on the line below each picture to tell what each character did.

1. Paul runs very fast.
   _____
   - - - - - - - - - - - - -

2. Kelly walks to the store.
   _____
   - - - - - - - - - - - - -

3. Dan sits in the park.
   _____
   - - - - - - - - - - - - -

4. The baby sleeps in her crib.
   _____
   - - - - - - - - - - - - -

Try this: Choose one character. Write about his or her day.

Name _____

(character)

Picture This

Read the stories. Then draw the characters.

1. Jen has curly hair. She smiles a lot. Today, Jen lost a tooth. She wears a blue cap. Draw Jen.

2. Ruff is a puppy. Ruff has black spots. He has a red ball. Draw Ruff.

Try this: Circle the words that helped you draw the pictures.

Name _____

character

Trading Toys

Read the story problems. Find the answers.

1. John has three trucks, two balls, and one bear to trade. How many toys does John want to trade?

 _____

2. Pat has four bears. She has one baseball and one jump rope. How many toys does Pat want to trade?

 _____

3. Steve has one bear, seven balls, and two cars. How many toys does Steve have?

 _____

4. Terry has six dolls. She also brought five bears. How many toys did she bring?

 _____

5. Terry gave Pat two dolls. Pat gave Terry one ball. How many dolls does Terry have left?

 _____

6. John wanted a car. He gave Steve two balls and one truck. Steve gave John one car. How many trucks does John have now?

 _____

© Instructional Fair • TS Denison   IF5635 Story Elements

Name _____

Trading Toys (cont.)

Use the stories on page 11 to circle the characters who brought each kind of toy.

Who brought?

dolls

trucks and cars

bears

balls

Look at the chart. Circle the answers.

1. How many characters brought bears?
   one   two   three   four

2. How many brought trucks and cars?
   one   two   three   four

3. How many characters brought dolls?
   one   two   three   four

© Instructional Fair • TS Denison   IF5635 Story Elements

Name _____

Who Said That?

Read each sentence. Write the character's name on the line.

1. "Hey! I am angry," said _____.

2. "That big dog may bite," said _____.

3. "It's my birthday," said _____.

4. "I am bored," said _____.

5. "My dog was hit by a car," said _____.

6. "That loud noise scared me," said _____.

7. "Mom and I are going to the beach," said _____.

8. "Don't push me!" said _____.

Try this: Write one more sentence for each character.

Name _____

character

Time for Dusty

Read the story. Answer the questions below.

Dusty wanted something. He ran to find Tyler. Tyler was reading a book. Dusty walked up the stairs to Holly's bedroom. She was playing a game. She did not look to see what Dusty wanted.

Dusty ran back down the steps. He picked up his leash.

He took the leash and went to Tyler. This time, Tyler put his book down. "What do you want, boy?" Tyler asked.

Dusty ran to the door. He wagged his tail.

Tyler pulled on his coat. He went to the steps and said, "Holly, do you want to go outside with us?"

"Yes," said Holly. She smiled.

1. Write the names of the characters. Circle the ones who are children.

   _____   _____   _____

2. What is Dusty?

   a boy   a dog   a cat   a girl

3. Circle the words that helped you guess what Dusty is.

   wagged his tail   picked up his leash   ran to the door

   Try this: Draw a picture of what might happen next.

character

The Lion and the Mouse

Read the story.

After eating a big meal, a lion took a nap. He woke up. Something ran across his back! He put out his big paw. It was a little mouse.

The mouse squeaked, "I am too small to be a good meal. Please let me go!"

"No!" roared the lion.

"Let me go. Someday I will help you," said the little mouse.

The lion laughed. "What could a tiny mouse do for a mighty lion?" But he was not hungry, so he let the mouse go.

The next day, the mouse heard a roar for help.

Hunters had trapped the lion. He was in a big net. The little mouse ran to the lion. She chewed the net with her sharp teeth. She chewed and chewed. The lion was free!

"Thank you," said the lion.

The lion and the mouse became good friends.

Name _____

The Lion and the Mouse (cont.)

Circle the right answers about *The Lion and the Mouse*.

1. The characters are

    kids   animals   cars

2. The characters are

    real   make-believe

3. Which character said "Please let me go"?

    lion   mouse

4. Which character said "What could a mouse do for me?"

    lion   mouse

5. Why did the lion let the little mouse go?

    He was kind.   He was not hungry.

6. Why did the mouse chew the lion's net?

    She was afraid.   She said she would help the lion.

Write the words that tell about each character next to its name.

Lion _____ _____ _____

Mouse _____ _____ _____

Word Bank
| big | small | sharp teeth |
| roars | squeaks | big paws |

Name _____

The Setting

Read and follow the directions.

The place a story happens is called the **setting**.

A setting can be a real place like a 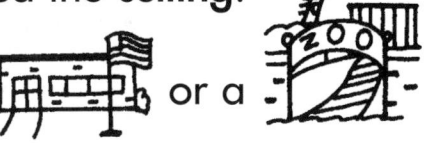 or a .

Sometimes stories take place in an  or even on the .

Sometimes the setting is make-believe.

Think about a story you like. What is the setting?

 the setting for a .

Draw a  around the setting for a .

Put an **X** on the setting for a .

Draw a line under the setting for a .

Try this: Draw a setting for a car.

Name _____

setting

In the Picture

Draw the setting around each character.

1.

2.

3.
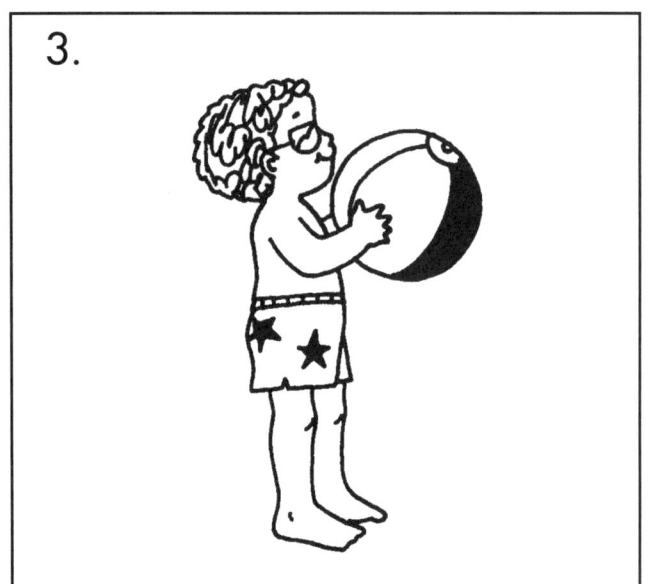

4.

Try this: Turn your paper over. Draw another setting for one of the characters on this page.

Name _____

Setting the Mood

setting

Settings can make you feel happy or sad.
Draw a line from each setting to how it makes you feel.

Happy

Sad

Try this: Draw a setting that makes you happy.

Name _____

setting

Out of Place

Cross out the picture that doesn't belong in each setting.

1. [school] — desk, books, cow, computer
2. [playground] — dinosaur, trash can, bench, squirrel
3. [Food-Mart] — fruit, horse, bread, shopping cart
4. [Zoo] — lion, monkey, giraffe, helicopter
5. [bedroom] — bed, toy boat/clown, tree, lamp

Name _____

setting

Get the Picture

Write the words from the Word Bank on the lines beside the setting where they belong.

Word Bank

| spider | cake | water | dog | cobwebs | balloons |
| ball | gift | cat | fish | towel | weeds |

1.
_____ _____

2.
_____ _____

3.
_____ _____

4.
_____ _____

Try this: Pick one setting. List three more things that belong there.

Name _____

setting

It's About Time

Sometimes the setting tells us *when* the story takes place. Read each clue. Write the correct clue letter on the month that matches each setting.

a. On a snowy day

b. At a Valentine's Day party

c. In a yard full of leaves

d. In a park with new flowers

e. Watching fireworks

f. In a kitchen, with a turkey cooking

Try this: Write all the months of the year in order.

Name _____

setting

Time Travel

Settings tell us if a story is set long ago, today, or in the future. Read each story sentence. When did each story take place? Draw an **X** in the right box.

long ago	today	future

1. Josh saw the covered wagons roll across the plains.

2. Tracy strapped on her helmet. She rode her bike along the trail.

3. Mark looked at the stars around him. He lived in a green pod. He rode a rocket bus to school.

4. It was Laura's first train ride. She watched the other wagons come to the station. The train moved slowly.

5. Zach's family parked their mini-van in the big lot. They crossed a red bridge to the zoo.

Try this: Circle clue words. Then draw a picture to show one of these settings.

Name _____

setting

Where Are We?

Read each paragraph. Write the setting on the line.

1. Chester was hungry. He ran down the tree trunk. He pawed at the dead leaves. He wanted the nut he had hid yesterday. He dug and dug. It wasn't there! He looked at all the other trees. Now, where did he hide that nut?

_____

2. Mark looked out the window. He could see Earth behind him. It looked very small from way out here. Then he looked at Pluto. That's where he was headed. He hoped he would like his new home.

_____

3. I sat down at my desk. I was in big trouble. I did my math last night. I put my paper in my backpack. But I didn't zip it all the way. On the way to school, a big bird landed on my head. He flew off with my paper. How will I tell Mr. Davis?

_____

Setting Bank

School   Outer Space   Forest

Name _____

setting

Birthday Money

Marcie has birthday money to spend. Count her money. Circle the most expensive item Marcie can buy at each store.

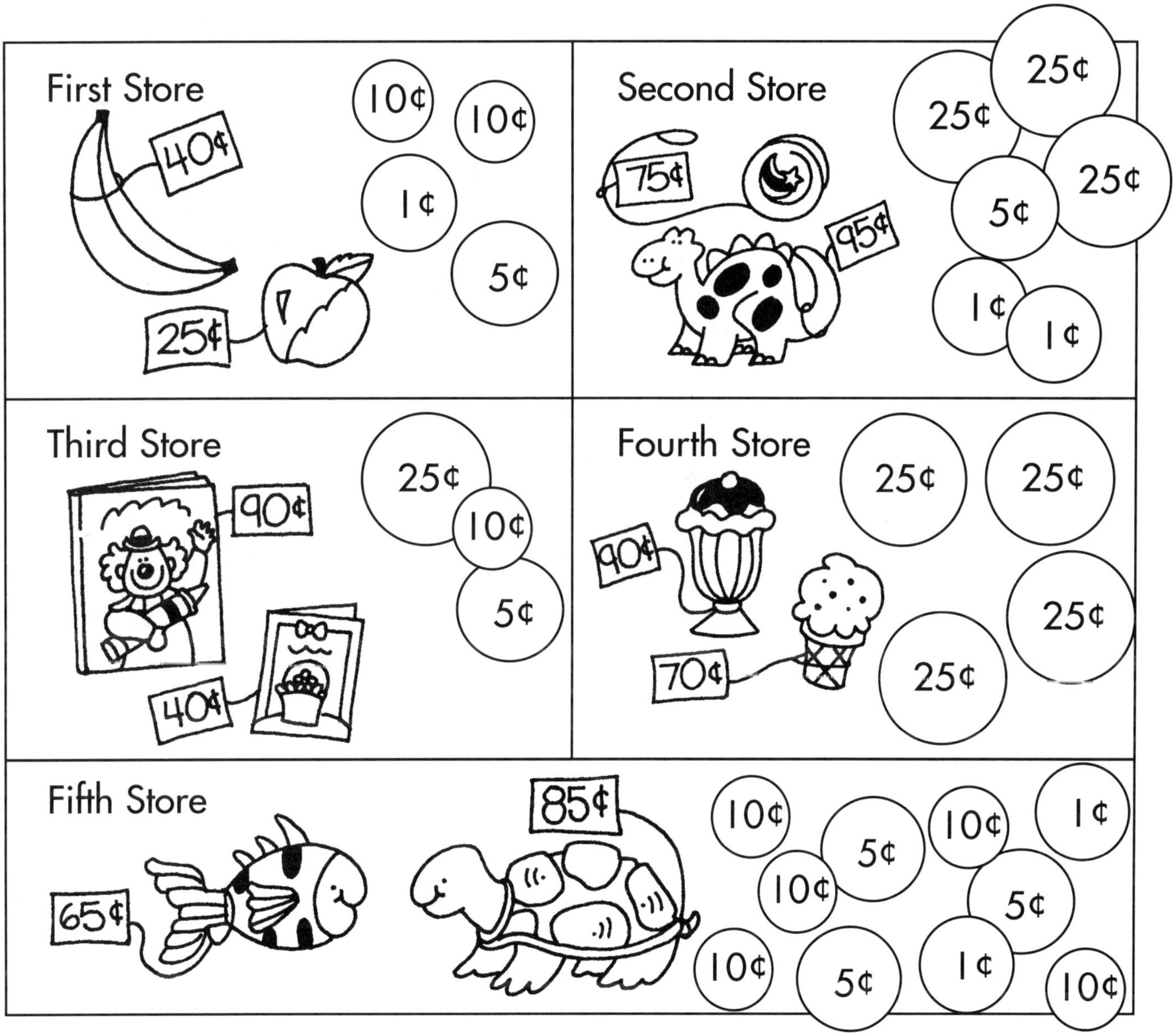

First Store — banana 40¢, apple 25¢ — coins: 10¢, 10¢, 1¢, 5¢

Second Store — dinosaur 75¢, yo-yo 95¢ — coins: 25¢, 25¢, 25¢, 25¢, 5¢, 1¢, 1¢

Third Store — book 90¢, card 40¢ — coins: 25¢, 10¢, 5¢

Fourth Store — sundae 90¢, ice cream cone 70¢ — coins: 25¢, 25¢, 25¢, 25¢, 25¢

Fifth Store — fish 65¢, turtle 85¢ — coins: 10¢, 10¢, 1¢, 5¢, 10¢, 5¢, 10¢, 5¢, 1¢, 10¢

Where would Marcie find all these stores? Choose the best setting for her shopping trip.

    her home   the mall   a farm

Name _____

Birthday Money (cont.)

> Write what Marcie bought at each store on page 25.
> Did she buy it first, second, third, fourth, or fifth?

Setting	What Marcie Bought	Order of Store
Toy Store		
Ice Cream Shop		
Grocery Store		
Pet Store		
Book Store		

List what Marcy bought in ABC order.

1. _____   4. _____

2. _____   5. _____

3. _____

Name _____

setting

Friends on the Map

When stories are about real places, you can find the settings on a map. Follow the directions below.

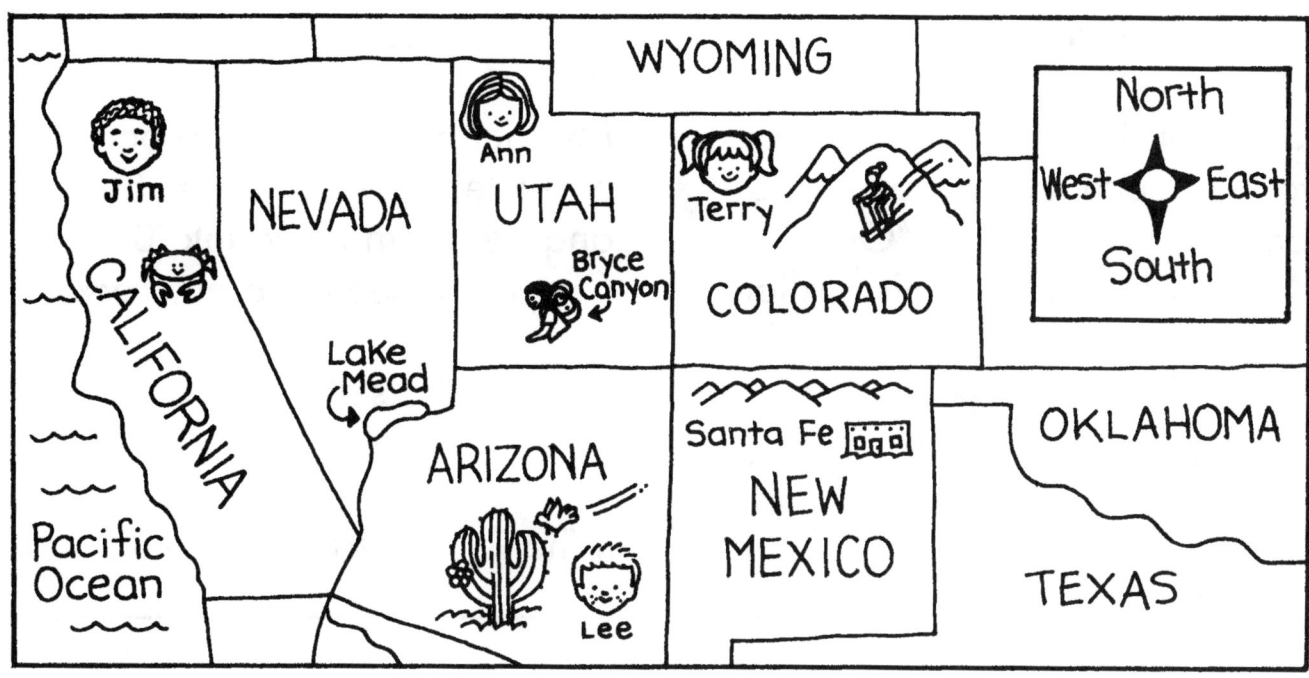

1. Color the state **west** of Nevada blue.

2. Color the state **south** of Utah red.

3. Color the state **north** of New Mexico green.

4. Color the state **east** of Nevada purple.

5. Color the other states yellow.

Try this: Write a story. Then draw a map that shows where your story happened.

© Instructional Fair • TS Denison   IF5635 Story Elements

Name _____

Friends on the Map (cont.)

Four children wrote stories about their friends. Read the stories. Look for clues. Use the map on page 27. Then answer the questions below.

Terry's Friend

One hot day, my friend walked to the beach. He waded into a pool. Then he yelled, "Ouch!" A little crab pinched his big toe.

What is the setting?
_____

Who is Terry's friend?
_____

Lee's Friend

My friend put on hiking boots and filled a water bottle. She and her mom hiked into Bryce Canyon to see the pretty rocks.

What is the setting?
_____

Who is Lee's friend?
_____

Jim's Friend

My friend has a special animal home in his backyard. It is a huge cactus. It has big arms. Lots of birds make nests in holes in the arms. My friend likes to watch the birds.

What is the setting?
_____

Who is Jim's friend?
_____

Ann's Friend

My friend's birthday was fun. She learned to snowboard. Her family drove to the mountains. It was cold. There was lots of snow. She learned to slide down the hills.

What is the setting?
_____

Who is Ann's friend?
_____

Name _____

setting

Science Poster

After a class trip, Tony and Jeff made a science poster. Can you guess where they went?

a. Tony punched holes in black paper.
b. Jeff drew a circle on yellow paper and cut it out.
c. Tony glued his black paper on white paper.
d. Jeff glued his yellow paper on the black paper.
e. Jeff found a picture of a telescope in a magazine.
f. Tony cut the picture out. He glued it to their poster.

Answer the questions.

1. What is the best title for the boys' poster?

    Star Watching   Art Day   Trips Are Fun

2. What setting did the boys make?

    a starry night   classroom   school bus

3. What did the students do on the trip?

    looked at stars and the moon   camped out

4. What science equipment did they use?

    microscope   telescope   magnifying glass

Try this: Make a poster like the one in the story.

Name _____

[problem]

What's the Problem?

Characters in stories have **problems** to solve.

A  wants a new , but Mom says no.

A  wants an , but she lost her money.

A hides a , but a  steals it.

The  needed a house that

the wolf could not blow down.

Look at the pictures below. Draw a line from each character to the problem in the story.

1.    He fell asleep and did not blow his horn.

2.    She had too many children.

3.    She was scared by a spider.

Try this: Draw a picture of the problem in "Mary Had a Little Lamb."

Name _____

problem

The Dog and the Bone

Look at the story. Circle the answers to each question.

1. The character is   a dog.   a bone.

2. The character wants   a drink of water.   the biggest bone.

3. The dog's problem is   he lost his bone.   he can't hold two bones in his mouth.

© Instructional Fair • TS Denison   31   IF5635 Story Elements

Name _____

(problem)

Beach Trouble

Polly Packrat had a bad day at the beach. Match the problems with the pictures in the maze. Then help poor Polly get home.

a. tripped on a rock   c. bitten by a crab   e. at home

b. sunburned her nose   d. lost her beach ball

Try this: Draw a picture showing one of Polly's problems.

Name _____

[problem]

Lots of Problems

Look at the books. The titles tell about each character's problem. Put an X on the picture that does not belong.

1.  *The Fox and the Grapes*

2.  *The Lost Balloon*

3.  *Too Many Kittens*

4.  *Bad Day at the Beach*

Try this: Write a sentence about one of the problems.

© Instructional Fair • TS Denison   33   IF5635 *Story Elements*

Name _____

(problem)

I Know an Old Lady

Some of the old lady's problems are mixed up! Read the story. Then use letters (a, b, c) to show the problems in the right order. The first one is done for you.

__a.__ 1. I know an 👵 who swallowed a 🪰 .

_____ 2. She swallowed the 🕷 to catch the 🪰 .

_____ 3. She swallowed a 🐶 to catch the 🐱 .

_____ 4. She swallowed a 🐦 to catch the 🕷 .

_____ 5. She swallowed a 🐱 to catch the 🐦 .

_____ 6. She swallowed a 🐄 to catch the 🐐 .

_____ 7. She swallowed a 🐐 to catch the 🐶 .

_____ 8. She swallowed a 🐴 to catch the 🐄 .

How in the world did she swallow a 🐴 ?

9. What was the old lady's first problem? _____

_____

10. How many animals did she swallow? _____

Name _____

I Know an Old Lady (cont.)

> Put the old lady's animals in the right order. Circle the right answer for each question.

1. The first animal that the  swallowed was a

2. The second animal that the  swallowed was a

3. The third animal that the  swallowed was a

4. The fourth animal that the  swallowed was a

5. The  also swallowed

> **Try this:** Draw a picture of the funniest problem.

Name _____

(problem)

Oh, No!

Write the letters on the lines to match each story to its picture.

1. John got his puppy's leash and walked back into the yard. Then he cried, "Oh, no!" ____

a.

2. John pulled on his boots, mittens, and hat. He got his sled and walked to the top of the hill. He looked at the hill. "Oh, no!" he sighed. ____

b.

3. Buster was very hungry. He had played ball with John all morning. He ran to his food bowl. Oh, no, panted the puppy. ____

c.

4. Mom wanted to cook eggs for breakfast. She took the carton out, then set it on the counter. Buster jumped up. The eggs fell. "Oh, no!" cried Mom. ____

d.

Name _____

(problem)

A Gift for Mama

Read the story. Answer the questions below.

Polly shook her piggy bank. It was empty. She had no money to buy Mama a gift for Mother's Day. The little packrat sat down on her bed. What could she do?

Then Polly smiled and hopped up. She pulled a big bag from under her bed. Mama had told her to throw it all away. Maybe she would not have to throw out these things.

This is what Polly took out of her bag:

three green buttons   one long piece of red ribbon
one blue feather   one brown basket

Polly went to work and soon she had a surprise for Mama.

1. Who is the main character? _____

2. What is her problem? _____

3. What is the story's setting? _____

4. Color the picture that shows what Polly made to solve her problem. Use the color clues you find in the story.

Name _____

problem

Who's Lost?

Read the story. Then answer the questions.

Marla looked into her pet's cage. Henry should have been asleep in his nest. But he wasn't there! Then Marla saw the open cage door. Henry was gone! But where did he go?

Marla looked all around the cage. She looked on the floor. She looked under her bed. She did not find him.

Marla felt like crying as she got dressed for school. She sat down to put on her shoes. First she put on the left shoe. Then she picked up the right shoe. It felt heavy. Guess who she found in her shoe?

1. Who are the characters? _____

2. What's Marla's problem? _____

3. Where does this story take place? _____

4. What did Marla find in her shoe? _____

5. Circle Henry:

Name _____

The Big Problem

(problem)

Read the story. Answer the questions on page 40.

Every day the cat chased the mice.

The mice had to hide in their nest.

They could not hunt for food.

They were very hungry.

"What can we do?" said Mother Mouse.

"I don't know," said the biggest mouse.

"I don't know," said the oldest mouse.

"I don't know," said the tallest mouse.

"I know," said the smallest mouse. "Let's hang a bell around the cat's neck. Then when we hear him coming, we can run."

Everyone cheered. They told the smallest mouse how smart she was.

Then the oldest mouse said, "That is a good idea, but we still have a problem. Who will put the bell on the cat?"

The Big Problem (cont.)

> Think about *The Big Problem*. Answer the questions.

1. Who are the characters in the story?

   five mice and a cat   five mice   five mice and a dog

2. What's the setting?

   in a school   in the mice's nest   in the forest

3. What is the problem at the beginning of the story?

   The cat laughs at the mice.   The cat keeps the mice from finding food to eat.

4. What character asked, "What can we do?"

   smallest mouse   Mother Mouse   oldest mouse

5. What characters said, "I don't know"?

   all the mice   the oldest, tallest, and biggest mice

6. What is the problem at the end of the story?

   _____

7. What is the best title for this story?

   Five Bad Mice   The Cat and the Mice   A Big Mouse

Name _____

mixed elements

The Snowman

Read the story. Then fill in the chart.

Bess lives in Arizona. Her best friend, Tyler, just moved to Michigan.

Tyler wrote to Bess and told her about his first snowman. He rolled a great, big snowball. He made a smaller one and set it on top of the big one. Then he made a smaller snowball for a head. Tyler used rocks to make eyes and a happy smile. He put his dad's fishing hat on the snowman's head.

Bess wanted to make a snowman, too. But it is too hot in Arizona for snow.

Bess had an idea. She put on Mom's work gloves. She picked up a big tumbleweed. She put a smaller tumbleweed on the bigger one.

Then she got a red potato, two olives, and her brother's cowboy hat. Bess went back outside. She used the two olives for eyes. She used the potato for a mouth. Then she put her brother's hat on top of the smaller tumbleweed.

Later, Bess wrote a letter to Tyler. She told him about her snowman that would never melt!

Snowman Part	Bess	Tyler
Mouth		
Eyes		
Hat		
Will it melt?		

Name _____

(plot)

Putting It All Together

(Let's review what you know!)

Stories are about **characters**. The characters usually have a **problem** to solve. The place the story happens is called the **setting**.

A story also needs something to happen. When characters try to solve their problems, everything that happens is a part of the **plot**. The plot is what moves the story along.

The story plot is often divided into three sections: the **beginning**, the **middle**, and the **end**.

The **beginning** of the story tells about the characters and the problem.

The **middle** of the story often tells how the character tries to solve the problem. Sometimes the character tries two or three things that don't work before finding the right answer.

The **end** of the story is when the character finally solves the problem.

When you put all three of these parts together, you have the story plot.

Putting it all Together (cont.)

Look at the stories. Label the **beginning**, the **middle**, and the **end** of the plot.

1. _____   _____   _____

2. _____   _____   _____

3. _____   _____   _____

plot

Casey the Cowgirl

Read the story.

Every morning, Casey puts on her jeans, boots, and cowboy hat. She wants to be a cowgirl like her Aunt Jessie. But she doesn't have a horse to ride. She tried to ride Bowser, the family's Great Dane. He just sat down. Casey slid off. Then Casey got on the back of the couch. She whooped and yelled until Mom came in.

"Get off the couch and be quiet," she said.

"I'm a cowgirl riding my horse, just like Aunt Jessie," Casey said.

Then Casey tried her roping. But she did not have any cows to rope, so she tried to rope her stuffed bear. She knocked over a lamp. It broke into pieces. Mom ran in to see what happened.

"Go to your room," she said.

"How will I ever learn to be a cowgirl like Aunt Jessie?" Casey asked.

The next week, Mom said, "I have a surprise. We are going out west to see Aunt Jessie."

"Great!" Casey said. "Now I can learn to be a real cowgirl with real horses, real cows, and Aunt Jessie!"

Name _____

Casey the Cowgirl (cont.)

Answer the questions about the story on page 44.

1. Who is the main character? _____

2. What is the setting? _____

3. What is Casey's problem? _____
_____

Answer the questions below to write a summary of the story.

4. What happened first? _____
_____

5. What happened second? _____
_____

6. How did the story end? _____
_____

7. Would you like to be Casey's friend? Why or why not?
_____
_____

Name _____

mixed elements

It's the End

Read the beginning and middle of each story.
Write your own ending.

1. Hoppy Hare and Tommy Tortoise lined up for the start of the race. Hoppy ran and ran. He was far ahead of Tommy. He sat down under a tree to take a nap.

   What happened? _____
   _____
   _____

2. A crow stole a piece of cheese from a picnic. She flew up in a tree to eat it. A hungry fox saw the crow. He wanted her cheese. He called to the crow, "Oh, pretty crow! Your feathers are shiny. If your voice is sweet too, then you must be a queen." The silly crow was tricked by the fox. She started to sing.

   What happened? _____
   _____
   _____

3. A boy tending the village sheep got bored. He wanted to play a trick. "Wolf, wolf!" he shouted. All the people in his village came running. They found the sheep safe and the boy laughing. The next day the same thing happened.

   What happened? _____
   _____
   _____

Answer Key

Characters Tell the Story..........4
1. Little Red Riding Hood, bottom
2. Goldilocks, top
3. Cinderella, center

Happy or Sad?..........5
1. sad face
2. happy face
3. happy face
4. sad face
5. sad face
6. happy face

It's My Story..........6
1. Lisa; Lisa Makes a Mask
2. Ramon; Ramon Flies a Kite
3. Ruff; Ruff Finds a Bone

The Hunters..........7
1. girl picture (Katie)
2. boy picture (Tom)
3. boy picture
4. girl picture
5. boy picture
6. both pictures

Name That Character!..........8
1. Gingerbread Boy
2. Itsy Bitsy Spider
3. Little Red Hen
4. Big Bad Wolf

Go, Characters, Go!..........9
Lines should be drawn to correct pictures.
1. runs
2. walks
3. sits
4. sleeps

Picture This..........10
Pictures should match descriptions.

Trading Toys..........11–12
1. 6
2. 6
3. 10
4. 11
5. 4
6. 2

Chart, page 11:
Line 1: Terry; Line 2: John and Steve;
Line 3: All; Line 4: John, Pat, Steve.
1. four
2. two
3. one

Who Said That?..........13
1. Chan
2. Mary
3. Keesha
4. Pedro
5. Ted
6. Mary
7. Keesha
8. Chan

Time for Dusty..........14
1. Dusty, Tyler (circled), Holly (circled)
2. a dog
3. wagged his tail, picked up his leash

The Lion and the Mouse..........15-16
1. animals
2. make-believe
3. mouse
4. lion
5. He was not hungry.
6. She said she would help the lion.
   Lion: big, roars, big paws
   Mouse: small, squeaks, sharp teeth

The Setting..........17
Castle circled; cave boxed; circus tent Xed; playground underlined.

In the Picture..........18
Appropriate settings should be drawn around characters.

Setting the Mood..........19
Happy: new bike; birthday party; beach scene; mother with cookies.
Sad: cat in tree; abandoned house; ripped toy; melting snowman.

Out of Place..........20
1. cow
2. dinosaur
3. horse
4. helicopter
5. tree

Get the Picture..........21
1. ball, water, towel
2. weeds, spider, cobwebs
3. cat, dog, fish
4. cake, balloons, gift

It's About Time..........22
January, a.; February, b.; May, d.; July, e.; October, c.; November, f.

Time Travel..........23
1. long ago
2. today
3. future
4. long ago
5. today

Where Are You?..........24
1. Forest
2. Outer Space
3. School

Answer Key (cont.)

Birthday Money 25–26

first store: apple; second store: yo-yo; third store: card; fourth store: sundae; fifth store: fish

She would find the stores in the mall.
Toy Store: yo-yo; second
Ice Cream Shop: sundae; fourth
Grocery Store: apple; first
Pet Store: fish; fifth
Book Store: card; third
1. apple
2. card
3. fish
4. sundae
5. yo-yo

Friends on the Map 27–28

1. California, blue
2. Arizona, red
3. Colorado, green
4. Utah, purple
5. Wyoming, New Mexico, Oklahoma, and Texas, yellow
Terry's Friend: California; Jim
Lee's Friend: Utah; Ann
Jim's Friend: Arizona; Lee
Ann's Friend: Colorado, Terry

Science Poster 29

1. Star Watching
2. a starry night
3. looked at stars and the moon
4. telescope

What's the Problem? 30

1. She had too many children.
2. He fell asleep and did not blow his horn.
3. She was scared by a spider.

The Dog and the Bone 31

1. a dog
2. the biggest bone.
3. he lost his bone.

Beach Trouble 32

Problems occur in this order in the maze: d; a; c; b; e.

Lots of Problems 33

1. X over pancake-flipping fox
2. X over clown with balloons
3. X over girl with sleeping puppy
4. X over boy at school desk

I Know an Old Lady 34–35

1. a.
2. b.
3. e.
4. c.
5. d.
6. g.
7. f.
8. h.
9. She swallowed a fly.
10. eight

On page 35, these pictures should be circled:
1. fly
2. spider
3. bird
4. cat
5. goat

Oh, No! 36

1. d.
2. b.
3. a.
4. c.

A Gift for Mama 37

1. Polly
2. no money for a gift
3. Polly's room
4. middle picture (hat) colored

Who's Lost? 38

1. Marla and Henry
2. Henry is missing
3. Marla's room

4. Henry
5. hamster circled

The Big Problem 39–40

1. five mice and a cat
2. in the mice's nest
3. The cat keeps the mice from finding food to eat.
4. Mother Mouse
5. Oldest, tallest, and biggest mice
6. who will put the bell on the cat
7. The Cat and the Mice

The Snowman 41

Chart filled in with Bess's details: mouth, potato; eyes, olives; hat, cowboy hat; no (it won't melt)
Tyler's details: mouth and eyes, rocks; hat, fishing hat; yes (it melts)

Putting It All Together 42–43

1. middle, beginning, end
2. middle, end, beginning
3. beginning, middle, end

Casey the Cowgirl 44–45

1. Casey
2. Casey's house
3. She wants to be a cowgirl.
4. Casey tried to ride Bowser. She used the couch as a horse.
5. She broke a lamp.
6. The family will visit Aunt Jessie in Arizona. Casey will be able ride real horses.
7. Answers will vary.

It's the End 46

1. Tommy won the race.
2. The crow dropped the cheese, and the fox ate it.
3. When a wolf really came, nobody ran when the boy cried "Wolf!"